Contents

CW00497599

Revision: Sets 1 to 5

Follow the arrows to write over each letter and say its sound.

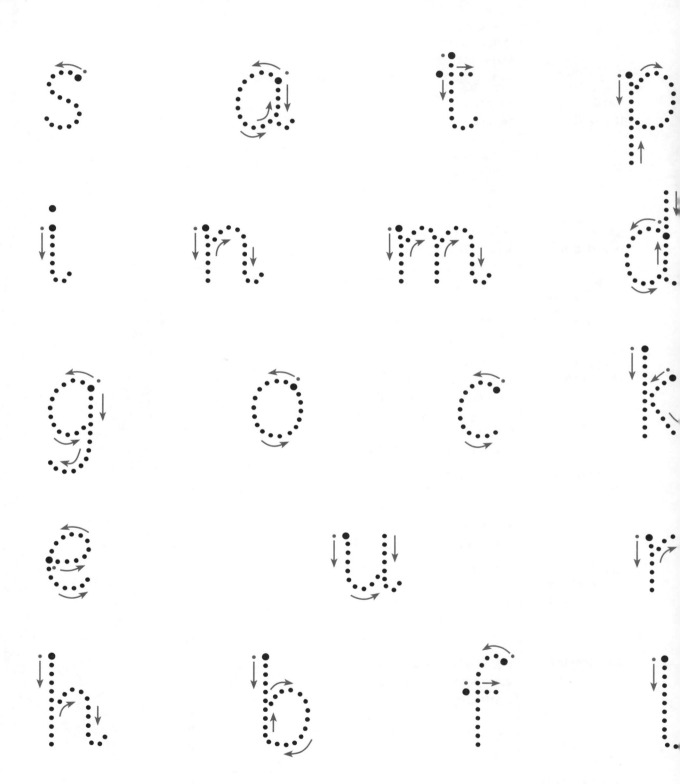

FOCUS • recognise letters as **graphemes** (the written representation of sounds) and say the sounds associated with them
• begin to form letter shapes

Blending for reading: Sets 1 to 5

Use **sound talk** to read the words on the boxes.
Press the **sound button** as you say the letter sound.
Then **blend** the sounds to say the word.

Join each word to its picture to show what it is in the box.

Segmenting for spelling: Sets 1 to 5

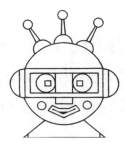

Say the words to go with these pictures.
Help Tog the robot to **sound talk** each word.
Break the word into separate sounds.

Draw rings around the letters that come next in each **phoneme** frame.

			a e u	p t g
n				

			i o u	p t g
d				

			a e i	p t g
c				

			a o u	m n r
s				

			e i o	p t g
k				

FOCUS ● **segment** (break up) words into separate phonemes (sounds)
          ● select letters to represent those phonemes

Word endings **ll**, **ss** and **ff**

Double letters are sometimes found at the end of a word.
The two letters make the same sound as the single letter.
Point to the double letters below and say the sounds.

ll   ss   ff

Read the words below. Say the sounds and **blend** them together.
Remember, double letters make one sound.
Join each word to its picture.

off

doll

puff

kiss

FOCUS   ● recognise that double letters (such as **ll**, **ss** and **ff**) make the same sound as the single letter
● blend words with double letters at the end

7

Word ending **ck**

▶ The letters **c** and **k** are found together at the end of some words.
The two letters make the same sound as **c** or **k** alone.
Say the single sound **ck**.

ck

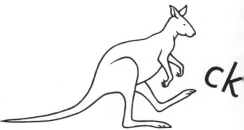

▶ Write **ck** on the end of each word below.
Read the words by saying the sounds and **blending** them.
Join each word to its picture.

ti c k ____

sa c k ____

so c k ____

lo c k ____

FOCUS ● know that **ck** at the end of words makes the same sound as **c** or **k**
● say the sounds and **blend** them in order to read words ending with **ck**

Reading sentences: tricky word **no**

Read this **tricky word**.

no

Read each question and write in the answer.

Can a cat hop?	no
Can a duck kick?	_____
Can a dog hum?	_____
Can a pig peck?	_____
Can a rock tell?	_____
Can a bell puff?	_____

Reading sentences: tricky word I

Read this **tricky word**.

I

Read the sentence.
Choose the word that makes sense.
Draw a ring round it.

I can run and _____. sick back kick

I got in a _____. mess miss moss

I huff and I _____. puff off cuff

I ran up a _____. till hill sell

I ran to a _____. rock pack back

FOCUS • practise reading the tricky word **I**
• practise reading the **high-frequency words can, and** and **in**
• sound and **blend** words for reading

The letter j

▶ Say the letter sound.

j

▶ Point to each letter and say the sound.

▶ Join the letter below to the things that begin with this sound.

The letter v

▶ Say the letter sound.

▶ Point to each letter and say the sound.

V   V   V

▶ Draw a ring round each thing that begins with this sound.

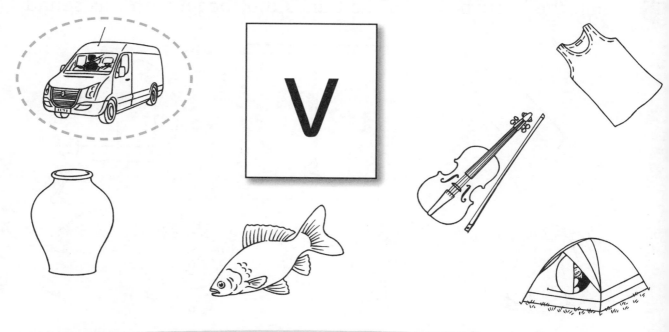

FOCUS   ● recognise the letter **v** and say the sound that it represents
                 ● select words that start with that sound

The letter w

▶ Say the letter sound.

W

▶ Point to each letter and say the sound.

W   W   W

▶ Colour each thing below that begins with this sound.

 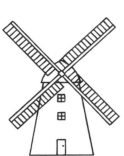  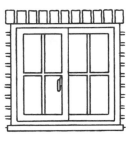

 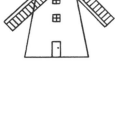  

The letter x

▶ Say the letter sound.

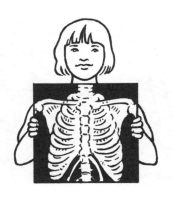

▶ Point to each letter and say the sound.

▶ Draw a ring round each thing with an **x** sound in it.

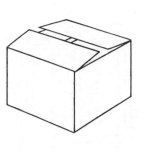   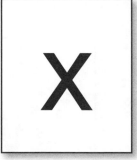   

FOCUS ● recognise the letter **x** and say the sound that it represents
                ● select words that have that sound in them

Blending for reading: Set 6

Use **sound talk** to read the words on the balloons.
Press the **sound button** as you say the letter sound.
Then **blend** the sounds to say the word.

Some of the words are real and some are made up.
Colour the balloon if the word on it is a real word.

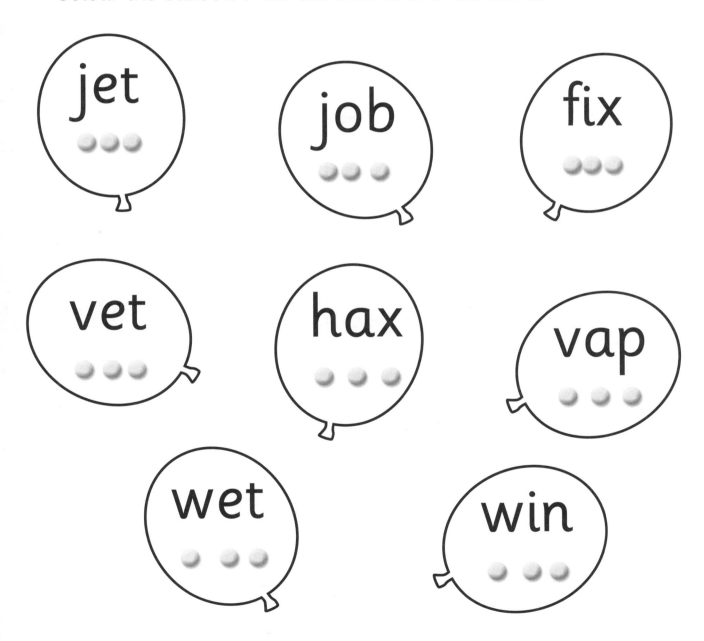

FOCUS ● say letter sounds and blend them in order to read words (**blending for reading**)

Segmenting for spelling: Set 6

◗ Say the words to go with these pictures.
Help Tog the robot to **sound talk** each word.
Break the word into separate sounds.

◗ Draw rings around the letters needed.

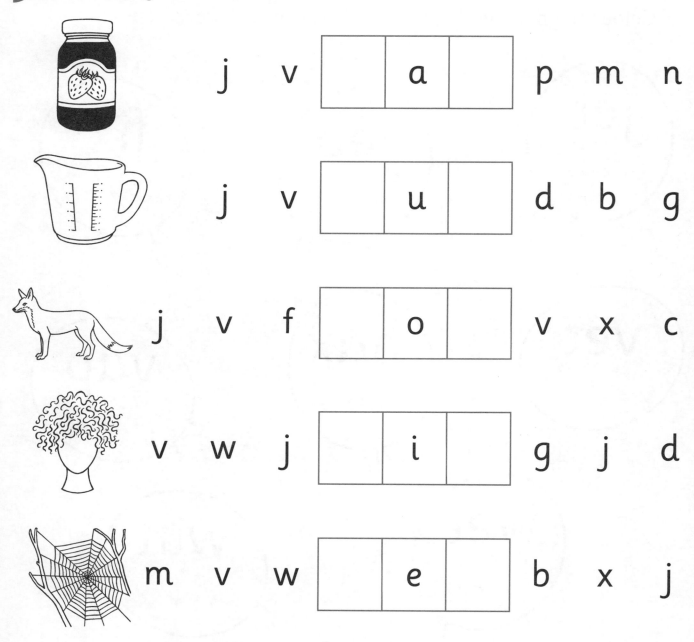

j v [| a |] p m n

j v [| u |] d b g

j v f [| o |] v x c

v w j [| i |] g j d

m v w [| e |] b x j

FOCUS • **segment** words into separate **phonemes** (segmenting for spelling)
• select letters to represent those phonemes

Reading sentences: **go**, **the** and **to**

▶ Read these **tricky words**.
Look out for the tricky letters as you say the letter sounds.

go   the   to

▶ Read each sentence.
Choose the word that makes sense.
Draw a ring round it.

The wig is in the ___.   boss   box   bop

I go up the ___.   hull   hiss   hill

Vic will go to ___.   bed   deb   bell

Can Max go to ___?   peck   pack   puck

The men go to the ___.   six   fix   van

FOCUS ● practise reading sentences with the tricky words **go**, **the** and **to**
   ● practise reading the **high-frequency words can, in, is** and **will**
   ● sound and **blend** unfamiliar words to read sentences (**blending for reading**)

17

The letter y

▶ Say the letter sound.

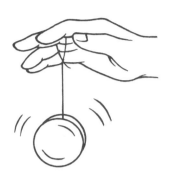

y

▶ Point to each letter and say the sound.

y   y   y

▶ Join the letter below to the things that begin with this sound.

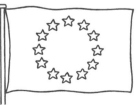

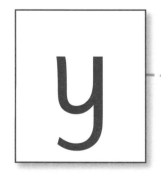

y

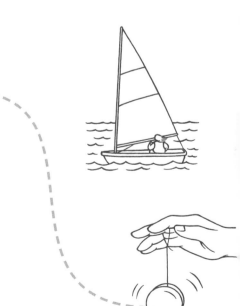

FOCUS   ● recognise the letter **y** and say the sound that it represents
● select words that start with that sound

The letters **z** and **zz**

▶ Say the letter sound.

▶ Point to each letter and say the sound.

z   z   z

▶ Draw a ring round each thing that begins with this sound.

   z

The letters **q** and **u**: **qu**

The letter **q** always has the letter **u** after it.

▶ Say the letter sound.

qu qu quack

▶ Point and say the sound.

qu   qu   qu

▶ Join the letters below to the things that begin with this sound.

qu

FOCUS ● recognise the letter **q** and say the sound that it represents
● select words that start with that sound

Blending for reading: Set 7

▶ Use **sound talk** to read these words.
Say each letter sound in turn.
Then **blend** the sounds to say the word.

▶ Join each word to the picture of the thing that makes that noise.

buzz

quack

fizz

yap

FOCUS • remember that two letters sometimes make one sound
• say and blend sounds in order to read words (**blending for reading**)

21

Revision: Sets 3 to 7

Follow the arrows to write over each letter and say its sound.

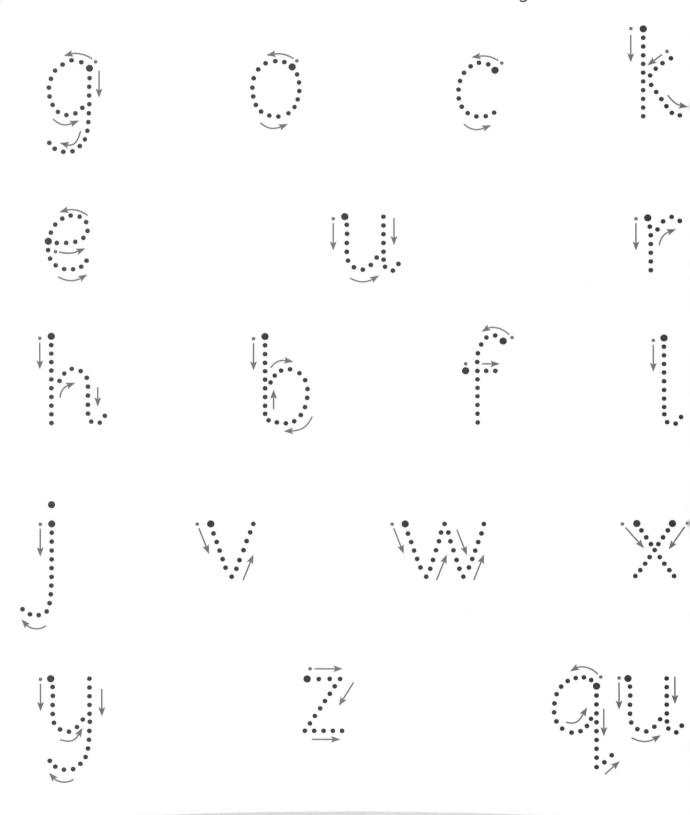

FOCUS ● recognise all the letters and say the sound associated with each one
● begin to form letters correctly

Reading sentences: **can**, **is**, **will**, **get**

Read each question.
Draw a ring round the right answer.

Is the sun wet?   yes   no

Can a vet fix a bus?   yes   no

Will a dog buzz?   yes   no

Can a duck quack?   yes   no

Will a jet be quick?   yes   no

Is a fox a pet?   yes   no

Can I jog to get fit?   yes   no

Has a box got a zip?   yes   no

FOCUS   ● sound and **blend** words for reading
● recognise the **high-frequency words can, is, will** and **get**
● recognise the **tricky words the** and **to**

23

Letter names 1

Sing this alphabet song to the tune of 'Twinkle, twinkle little star'. Point to the letters as you say the **letter names**.

a b c d e f g

h i j k l m n o p

q r s t u and v

w x y and z

Now we know the A B C

You can sing along with me.

FOCUS ● begin to learn the letter names by singing an alphabet song and pointing to the letters

The sound **sh**

▶ A **grapheme** is the written representation of a sound.
Sometimes two letters represent one sound.
Say the sound.

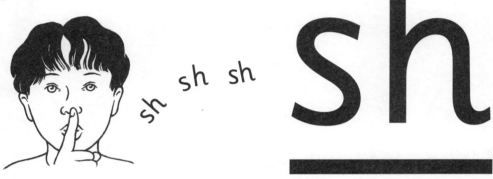

▶ Point and say the sound.

sh   sh   sh

▶ Join the card below to the things that begin with this sound.

FOCUS • recognise the **consonant digraph sh** and say the sound that it represents
• select words that start with that sound

25

The sound ch

▶ These two letters together make one sound.
Say the sound.

ch

▶ Point and say the sound.

ch ch ch

▶ Join the card below to the things that begin with this sound.

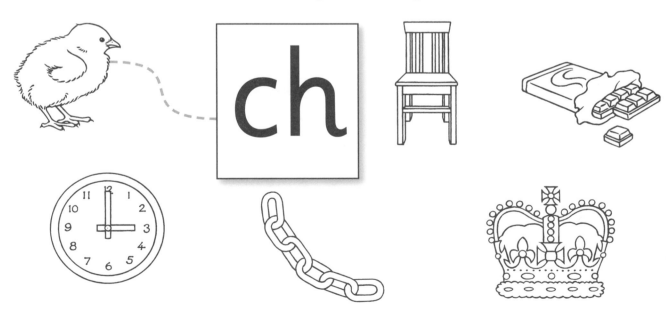

FOCUS • recognise the **consonant digraph ch** and say the sound that it represents
• select words that start with that sound

Blending for reading: sh

▶ Use **sound talk** to read the words on the fish.
Say the letter sounds.
Then **blend** the sounds to say the word.

▶ Some of the words have **sh** in them and some do not.
Colour the fish if the word has **sh** in it.

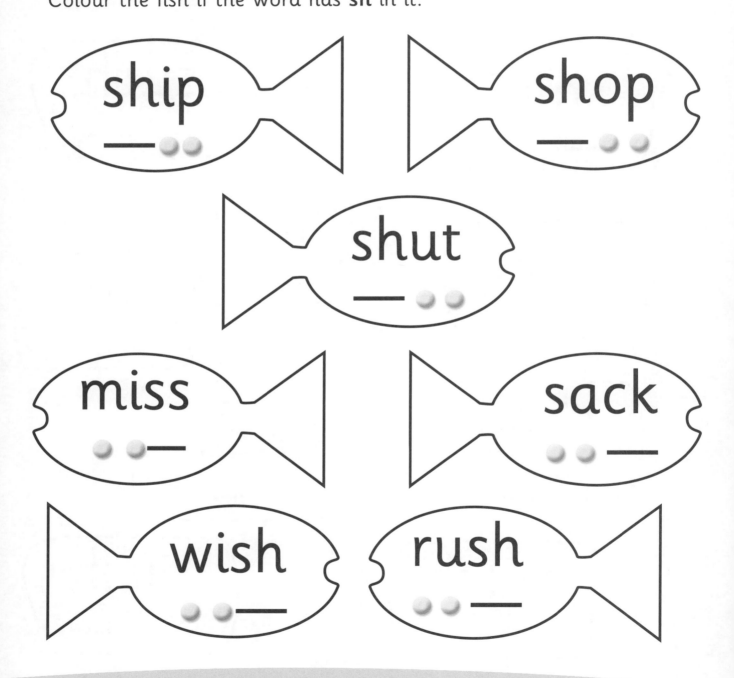

FOCUS • recognise in words the **consonant digraph sh** and say the sound that it represents
• blend words, remembering that two letters sometimes make a single sound

27

Blending for reading: ch

◗ Use **sound talk** to read the words on the chips.
Say the letter sounds.
Then **blend** the sounds to say the word.

◗ Some of the words have **ch** in them and some do not.
Colour the chip if the word has **ch** in it.

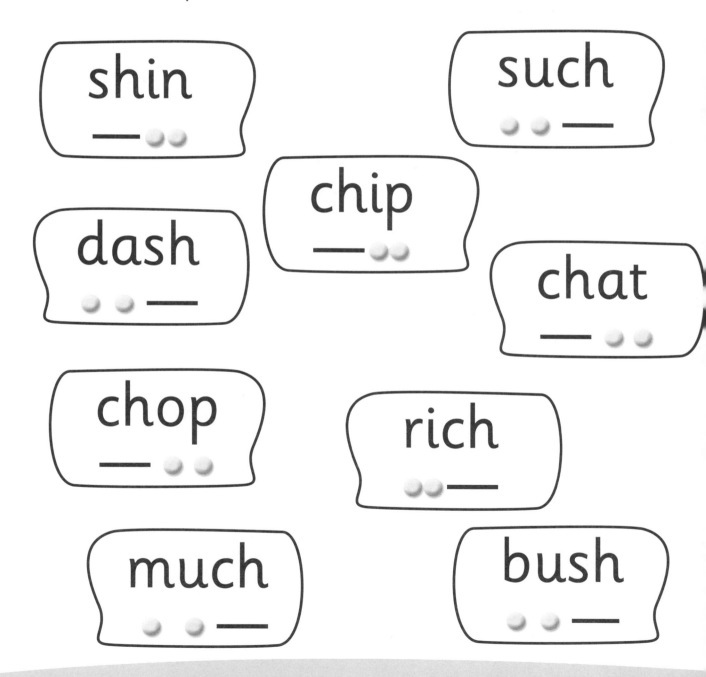

FOCUS ● recognise in words the **consonant digraph ch** and say the sound that it represents
● blend words, remembering that two letters sometimes make a single sound

Segmenting for spelling: **sh** and **ch**

▶ Say the words to go with these pictures.
Say each word in **sound talk**.
Break the word into separate sounds.

▶ Draw rings around the letters needed.

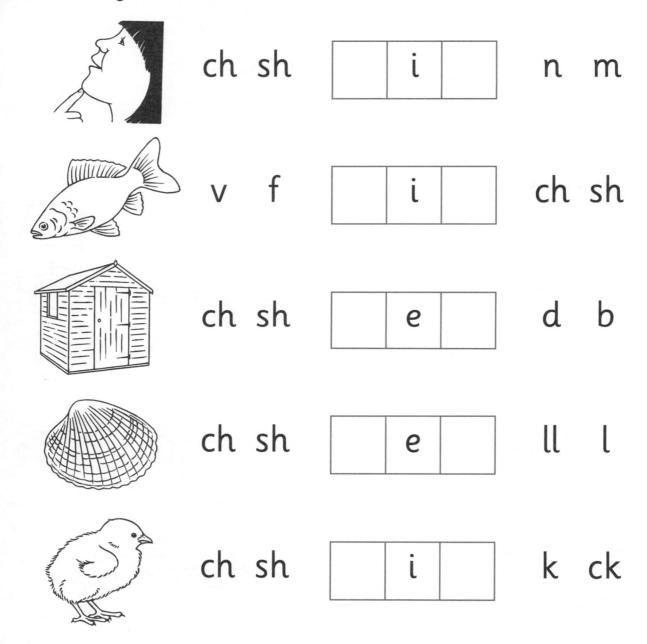

ch sh ▢ i ▢ n m

v f ▢ i ▢ ch sh

ch sh ▢ e ▢ d b

ch sh ▢ e ▢ ll l

ch sh ▢ i ▢ k ck

FOCUS • **segment** words into separate **phonemes** (segmenting for spelling)
• select letters to represent those phonemes

29

Reading: tricky words **he** and **she**

▶ Read these **tricky words**.
Look out for the tricky letter **e** when you say the letter sounds.

he   she

▶ Read about Mick and Tess.

Mick has a van.
It will not go.
Can he fix it?
Yes he can.

Tess has a ship.
It will not go.
Can she fix it?
Yes she can.

FOCUS ● recognise the tricky words **he** and **she**
● recognise the **high-frequency words will, can, not** and **it**
● sound and **blend** other words (**blending for reading**)

The sound th

▶ These two letters together make one sound.
Say the sound.

th

▶ Point and say the sound.

th   th   th

▶ Draw a ring round each thing that begins with this sound.

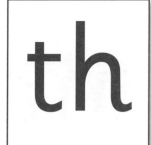

th

FOCUS ● recognise the **consonant digraph th** and say the sound that it represents
● select words that start with that sound

31

The sound **ng**

▶ These two letters together make one sound.
Say the sound.

▶ This sound comes at the ends of words.
Join the card below to the things that end with this sound.

FOCUS ● recognise the **consonant digraph ng** and say the sound that it represents
● select words that end with that sound

Blending for reading: **th** and **ng**

Use **sound talk** to read the words on the balloons.
Press the **sound button** as you say the sound.
Then **blend** the sounds to say the word.

Some of the words are real and some are made up.
Colour the balloon if the word on it is a real word.

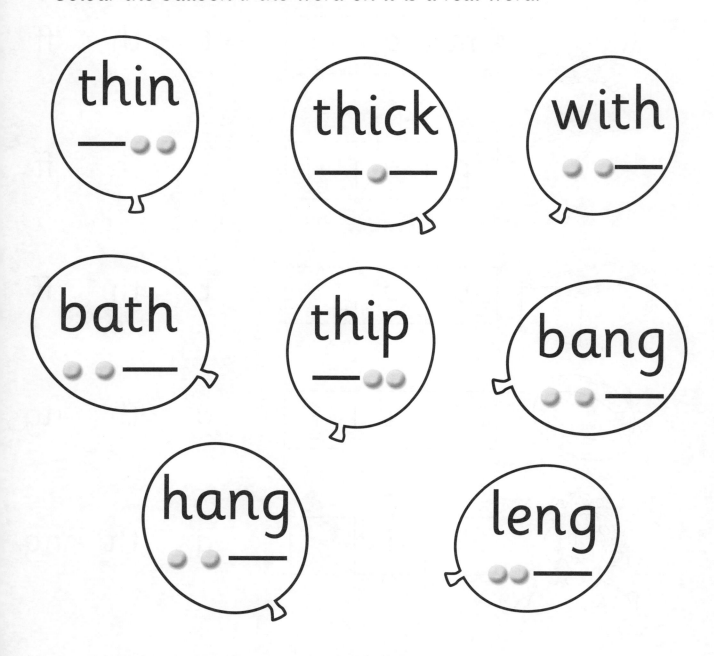

Segmenting for spelling: **th** and **ng**

Say the words to go with these pictures.
Say each word in **sound talk**.
Break the word into separate sounds.

Draw rings around the letters that should come next.

m	o	

t   th   ff

p	a	

t   th   ff

b	a	

t   th   ff

r	i	

g   th   ng

k	i	

g   th   ng

FOCUS • **segment** words into separate **phonemes**
• select letters to represent those phonemes

Letter names 2

Chant the cheerleaders' abc.
Point to the letters as you say the **letter names**.

a b c d e

Say the letter names with me

f g h i j

Say those letter names all day

k l m n o

Letter names are go, go, go

p q r s t

Say the letter names with glee

u v w x y z

Say those letter names in your head.

FOCUS ● learn the letter names by saying an alphabet rhyme and pointing to the letters

Reading clues: **with**, **this** and **them**

▶ Use **sound talk** to read these words.
Press the **sound buttons** and say each sound in turn.
Then **blend** the sounds to say the word.

this   with   them

▶ Read each clue.
Choose the correct answer.
Draw a ring round it.

I run on them   legs   pegs webs

I can hit with this   bit   bat   back

this has thin wings   fox   pig   moth

a shop can sell them   socks yells kicks

a fish has them   wings legs   fins

FOCUS ● practise reading the **high-frequency words this, with** and **them**
        ● sound and blend other words for reading
        ● read words with plural **s**

Segmenting for spelling: **ch**, **sh**, **th**, **ng**

Tog the robot has put the wrong letter or letters in one part of each **phoneme** frame below. Change the letters to make the word correct.

sh

| ~~ch~~ | i | p |

| r | i | g |

| th | i | ck |

| w | i | g |

| ch | e | d |

FOCUS • **segment** words into separate phonemes
• select letters to represent those phonemes, remembering that two letters sometimes make a single sound

37

Reading questions: **we**, **me** and **be**

Read these **tricky words**.
Look out for the tricky letter **e** when you say the letter sounds.

we   me   be

Read these questions.
Draw a ring round the right answer.

Can we chop a big log?   yes   no

Can we sing a ship?   yes   no

Can a chick peck at me?   yes   no

Can a big fish be rich?   yes   no

Can a fox be in a den?   yes   no

FOCUS ● recognise the tricky words **we**, **me** and **be**
● recognise the **high-frequency words can**, **at** and **big**
● read questions, sounding and **blending** words where necessary

Reading words with two parts

This word has two parts.

zigzag  zig/zag

Say the **letter sounds** and **blend** the first part of the word.
Say the letter sounds and blend the second part of the word.
Put the two parts together to read the word.

zig zag   zigzag

Use **sound talk** to read these two-part words.
Join each word to its picture.

cob/web

sun/set

back/pack

lap/top

Reading captions: tricky word **my**

▶ Read this **tricky word**.
Look out for the tricky letter **y** when you say the letter sounds.

my

▶ Read these captions.
Join each caption to its picture.

Jack with my ship

Jill in my hat

My mum had a shock.

My dad and his shed

This is my fish.

FOCUS ● recognise the tricky word **my**
● practise reading the **high-frequency words in, is, with, had, this** and **and**
● read captions, sounding and blending other words where necessary

Assessment 1: sound check

Assessment 1 tests the child's knowledge of the letters and sounds introduced in this book. Check that the child can do the following.

1 Give the sound when you point to each **grapheme**.

2 Point to the grapheme when you say the sound.

You should also run through again the letters learned earlier, as shown on page 4 of this book and on page 44 of **Sound Phonics** Phase Two.

ff	ll	ss
ck	j	v
w	x	y
z	qu	ch
sh	th	ng

Assessment 2: blending check

Assessment 2 checks the child's **blending for reading** using simple **CVC words**. Ask the child both to say the sounds and then **blend** them to make each word.

yet	jag	vat	tax
wax	well	yuck	quit
jazz	rang	chill	shell

shock	check
rung	thick

Assessment 3: segmenting check

Assessment 3 checks the child's **segmenting for spelling**. Ask the child to help you spell the word to go with each picture. Ask him or her to say the word in **sound talk** and tell you what letters to write.

Assessment 4: word check

1 These are some of the **tricky words** introduced so far. Ask the child to read them. By now he or she should be starting to read some of them automatically.

the	to	I	no	go
he	she	we	me	be

2 These are some of the **high-frequency words** introduced so far. Ask the child to read them. By now he or she should be starting to read some of them automatically.

at	is	it	in	can

not	get	will
this	with	them

Assessment 5: tracing letters check

Ask the child to write over each letter, using the arrows for guidance.

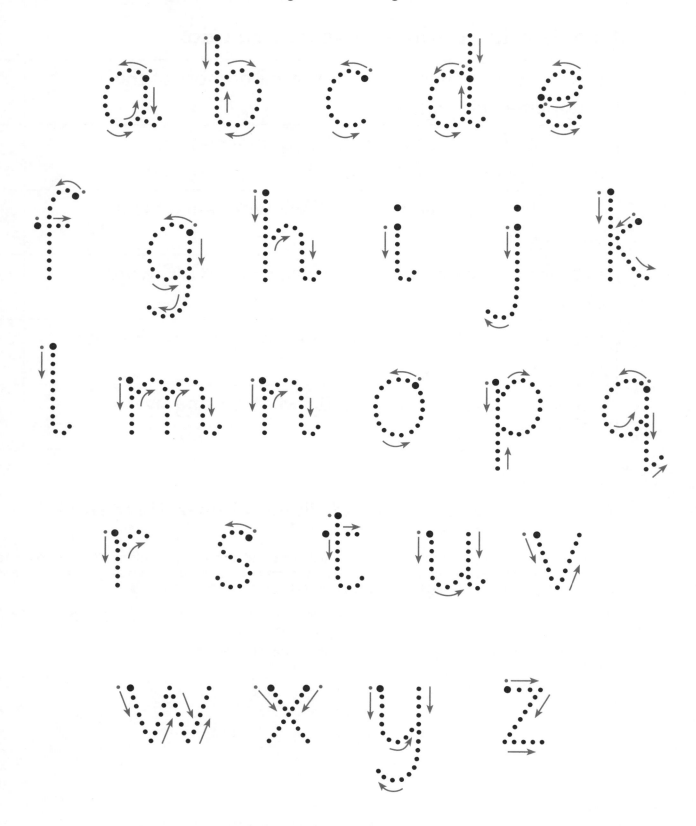

Assessment statements

Run through with the child these assessment statements.

Here is a list of the things you can do.

I can say the sound when shown all or most of the **graphemes** on page 41.	
I can point to all or most of the graphemes on page 41 when given the sound.	
I can **blend** and read simple **CVC words** like those on page 42.	
I can break down and try to spell simple CVC words like those on page 43.	
I can read the **tricky words the**, **to**, **I**, **no**, **go**, **he**, **she**, **we**, **me**, **be** and **my**.	
I can form each letter correctly when writing over it.	

What next?

You are now ready for **Sound Phonics Phase Three Book 2**.

Some children may not have fully grasped the skills of **blending** and **segmenting** CVC words but know all the graphemes introduced so far. Blending and segmenting continues throughout Phase Three so you can still progress to **Sound Phonics** Phase Three Book 2.

There may be a few letters that the child continues to confuse. Make a note of these and continue to practise them.

Keep using the alphabet song and chant to practise the **letter names**.

Glossary and notes for parents

blend	to say the separate sounds in a word and merge them to make the whole word
	Blending is the reverse of **segmenting**. **Blending for reading** involves looking at a word, recognising the letters, saying the letter sounds and blending them to read the word. In Phase Three, children learn to blend words where two letters represent one sound (**ch, sh, ck**).
consonant digraph	two consonants making one **phoneme** (**sh, ch, th, ng**)
CVC word	a word consisting entirely of three phonemes: a consonant (C) then a vowel (V) and a second consonant (C) (**cat, sun, rang**)
grapheme	a letter or sequence of letters representing a **phoneme**
high-frequency words	common words frequently found in children's reading material and used by them in their own writing
	Children read many **high-frequency words** by saying the letter sounds and blending them (**will, back, with**). With practice, children read these words automatically.
letter names	each letter has both a sound and a name – and children are taught letter sounds first as these help with reading and spelling; in Phase Three they learn letter names (see pages 24 and 35)
phoneme	one of the separate sounds that a word contains
segment	to break a word into separate sounds in order to spell it
	Segmenting is the reverse of **blending**. **Segmenting for spelling** involves breaking words into separate sounds and choosing the letters that make those sounds in order to spell the word.
sound button	a dot appearing below each letter, which the child presses as he or she says the letter sound; where two letters make one sound, a single line replaces the dots
sound talk	the process of saying, in the correct order, each **phoneme** in a word
	In Phase Three, children need to remember that two letters sometimes make one sound (**ll, ck, sh**). Where this is the case, you will see a line under the letters instead of the usual **sound button**.
syllable	one part of a word, usually containing one vowel sound
tricky words	words with letters that make unusual or unfamiliar sounds
	He, she, we, me and **be** are **tricky words** because the sound made by the letter **e** does not match the sound that children know for this letter. Children need to recognise tricky words, which can hamper reading.

Schofield&Sims

the long-established educational publisher specialising in maths, English and science

Sound Phonics prepares children for full fluency in reading, writing and spelling by providing intensive practice in phonics. A comprehensive phonics resource, it is fully compatible with *Letters and Sounds*, making it an ideal companion to this Government programme. **Sound Phonics** is equally suitable for use alongside any other incremental phonics teaching scheme.

The **Sound Phonics** activities reinforce children's early literacy skills through listening and speaking. From an early stage, children are encouraged to look at and point to letters – and gradually to trace and form them correctly. They also practise identifying and saying the correct sounds in words ('segmenting for spelling') and blending these sounds to read words ('blending for reading'), slowly moving on to segmenting and blending longer words. Children also practise reading and spelling 'tricky' words.

The first book in the series is a reusable stimulus book (**Sound Phonics Phase One**), which is designed for children in the Early Years Foundation Stage (EYFS). It is followed by nine one-per-child activity books for EYFS and Key Stage 1, which cover the developmental stages that *Letters and Sounds* refers to as Phases Two to Six. All the books in the series are listed at the foot of this page.

Each activity book supports teachers and other adult helpers by providing:

- integrated revision of points covered earlier
- 'Focus' statements, summarising the main objectives of every page
- assessment activities and an assessment summary
- explanatory notes
- a glossary of phonics terminology.

In **Sound Phonics Phase Three**, the child practises letter Sets 1 to 7 and is introduced to the concept of two or more letters making a single sound. The child works towards correct letter formation by tracing over enlarged letters, with arrows for guidance. 'Sound buttons', which help the child to say and then blend the sounds in a word, continue to support reading. 'Phoneme frames' are used to support segmenting for spelling.

Sound Phonics Phase Three Book 1, the third book in the series, focuses on:

- revising letter Sets 1 to 5
- practising letter Sets 6 and 7, plus four consonant digraphs
- practising letter names, using rhymes.

Help every child to tune into literacy with this reliable and accessible series.

ISBN 978-07217-1146-1

9 780721 711461

MIX
Paper from responsible sources
FSC® C010219

ISBN 978 07217 1146 1
EYFS & Key Stage 1
Age range 4–7 years

£3.50 (Retail price)

For further information and to place your order visit
www.schofieldandsims.co.uk or telephone 01484 607080